PENGUIN BOOKS

THE LIFE TREE

A.P.J. Abdul Kalam (1931–2015) was one of India's most distinguished scientists. He was responsible for the development of India's first satellite launch vehicle, the SLV-3, and the development and operationalization of strategic missiles. As chairman of the Technology Information, Forecasting and Assessment Council, he pioneered India Vision 2020, a road map for transforming India into an economically developed nation by 2020, focusing on PURA (Provision of Urban Amenities in Rural Areas) as a development system for countrywide implementation.

Kalam held various positions in the Indian Space Research Organisation and the Defence Research and Development Organisation and became principal scientific adviser to the Government of India, holding the rank of a cabinet minister.

The President of India between 2002 and 2007, Kalam was awarded honorary doctorates from thirty-eight universities and the country's three highest civilian honours—Padma Bhushan (1981), Padma Vibhushan (1990) and Bharat Ratna (1997).

Kalam authored fifteen books on a variety of topics that have been translated into many languages across the world. His most significant works are *Wings of Fire*, *India 2020: A Vision for the New Millennium*, *Target 3 Billion* and *Beyond 2020: A Vision for Tomorrow's India*.

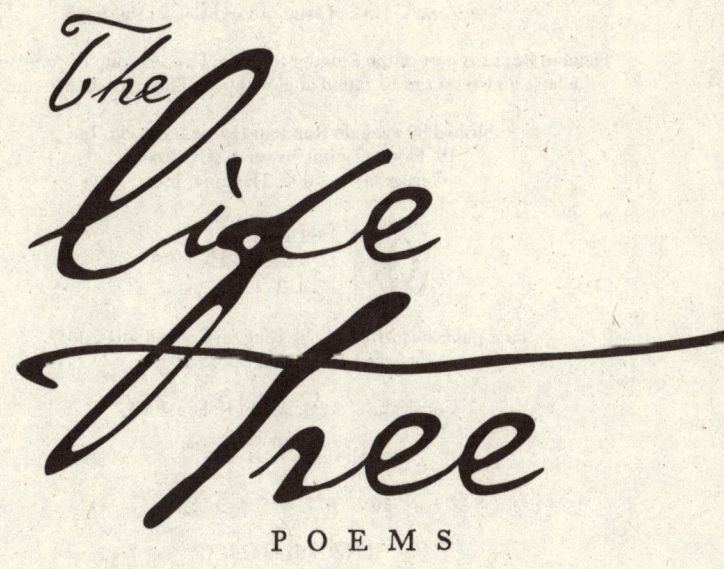

The Life Tree

POEMS

A.P.J. ABDUL KALAM

PENGUIN BOOKS

An imprint of Penguin Random House

PENGUIN BOOKS

USA | Canada | UK | Ireland | Australia
New Zealand | India | South Africa | China | Singapore

Penguin Books is part of the Penguin Random House group of companies
whose addresses can be found at global.penguinrandomhouse.com

Published by Penguin Random House India Pvt. Ltd
4th Floor, Capital Tower 1, MG Road,
Gurugram 122 002, Haryana, India

Penguin
Random House
India

First published in Viking by Penguin Books India 2005
Published in Penguin Books 2015

10 9 8 7 6 5 4 3 2

ISBN 9780143425847

Typeset in Sabon by S.R. Enterprises, New Delhi

Printed at Repro India Limited

www.penguin.co.in

Contents

There's only one corner of the universe you can be certain of improving, and that's your own self.

—Aldous Huxley

Acknowledgements

I have always admired the poetic eminence of Shri Atal Bihari Vajpayee. He spent a good amount of time in reading this collection and has quoted from these poems also in his characteristic and beautiful foreword. I thank him for his gracious gesture, in writing foreword for this book. I am grateful to Smt. Mani Darshi for translating some of these poems from the Tamil original. My thanks also to Shri Manav Gupta, for illustrating some of these poems so beautifully. I deeply appreciate Shri Krishan Chopra of Penguin Books for his patience in bearing with the delay of about two years and persisting with his painstaking efforts in bringing out this beautiful edition.

A.P.J. Abdul Kalam
4 December 2004

Foreword
Poems of Love, Faith and Patriotism

Our respected President, Dr A.P.J. Abdul Kalam, has contributed invaluably to our country's progress in space research and defence technologies. However, he is not only an eminent scientist. He is also a sensitive and thoughtful poet. This confluence of scientific brilliance and poetic talent is truly unique.

The poems contained in this book bring out Dr Kalam's deep love for India and her rich culture. Together with his devotion to God and to his Motherland, his devotion to humanity is also uniquely manifested in these poems. Believing his ability and achievements to be God's gifts, he has dedicated them to the welfare of the Indian people. Through the medium of his poetry he has sent a message of selfless service, dedication and pure faith.

Dr Kalam has always been an opponent of communalism, casteism, linguistic chauvinism, regionalism and violence. Showing a profound understanding of Indian society, he attempts to find solutions to problems with compassion, detachment, forbearance and sympathy. In these poems he has attempted, very credibly, to express in simple terms even a concept as complex as the search for God.

'O creator of dreams,
Why do you keep searching for God?
Nature is His home, purity His abode
And Life is but His blessing!
Keep loving nature and care for its beings,
Then you can see divinity all over!'

As a true Indian, Dr Kalam is naturally distressed by the misuse of religion for ungodly ends. Nevertheless, he is confident that true faith in God and compassion for humankind can save us from the poison of communalism and casteism. He says:

> *The so-called educated separate our souls....*
> *They give not knowledge but hate and defeat;*
> *Tell others not to heed their unwanted advice,*
> *As the Almighty created all equal and free.*

Behind his scientific achievements and poetic works, Dr Kalam dreams of a better world for the children of India and the world. He says:

> *I have no house, only open spaces*
> *Filled with truth, kindness, desire and dreams:*
> *Desire to see my country developed and great,*
> *Dreams to see happiness and peace abound.*

Reading Dr Kalam's poems, my heart fills with patriotism, love and faith. With this same faith I am honoured to place these poems before you.

New Delhi
25 October 2003

ATAL BIHARI VAJPAYEE

Great aim leads to great thoughts.

Desire, when it stems from the heart and spirit, when it is pure and intense, possesses awesome energy. This energy is released into the ether each night, as the mind falls into the sleep state. Each morning it returns to the conscious state reinforced with the cosmic currents. That which has been imagined will surely and certainly be manifested. You can rely, young citizen, upon this ageless promise as surely as you can rely upon the eternally unbroken promise of sunrise... and of spring.

Song of Youth

As a young citizen of India,
Armed with technology, knowledge and love for my nation,
I realize, small aim is a crime.

I will work and sweat for a great vision,
The vision of transforming India into a developed nation,
Powered by economic strength and a strong value system.

I am one of the citizens of the billion;
Only the vision will ignite the billion souls.
It has entered into me

The ignited soul compared to any resource
Is the most powerful resource on the earth,
Above the earth and under the earth.

I will keep the lamp of knowledge burning
To achieve the vision—Developed India.
If we work and sweat for the great vision with ignited minds,
The transformation leading to the birth
Of a vibrant, developed India will happen.

I pray to the Almighty:
May the divine peace with beauty enter into our people;
Happiness and good health blossom in our bodies, minds and
    souls.

Am I alone?

I and my friend Prof. Vidyasagar travelled together by air from Hyderabad to Delhi. Our plane soared through an awesome landscape of layer upon layer of dense cloud. The magnificent spectacle moved our souls. Thereafter, when we were walking in the lawns at the Asiad Village Complex, the beauty of the nagphalli tree, laden with flowers, soaked our souls with a divine experience. I was provoked into writing The Life Tree.

The Life Tree

O my human race,
How were we born,
In the universe of near infinity,
Are we alone?

This is the question for humanity in this millennium.
I sought the help of our creator.
I was seeking an answer for the great
Question of creation, weighing heavy on
My mind as I am in my seventieth orbit
Around the sun, my little habitat, the star
Where my race has lived billions of years
And will live billions of years more, till the sun shines.

On the eventful day, I was flying
The earth below me, the human habitat
Vanished in the white river of cloud,
Silent, turbulent, yet free
Everywhere the divine splendour reflecting,
Above, the full moon with its magnificent might.
My heart melted, my friend and co-passenger,
Vidyasagar, joined me in watching the heavenly display.
The beauty entered into our soul
And blossomed happiness in our mind and body.
We human beings bowed to the heavenly answer.
We are not alone, billions of billions of lives
Of various forms spring forth in the planets
Of galaxy after galaxy.
Then the dawn of the divine message:

7

There was the divine echo in the full-moon night
From my creator.
Shaken, bewildered, filled with wonder,
The echo engulfed me and my race.
'You, the human race is the best of my creation,
You will live and live.
You give and give till you are united,
In human happiness and pain;
My bliss will be born in you.
Love is continuum,
That is the mission of humanity,
You will see every day in Life Tree.
You learn and learn
My best of creations.'

Beautiful morning it was,
Sun radiating, driving away the clouds;
Parrots and kokilas were at their musical flight.
We the yellow heaven group* entered
Flower garden of Asiad.
Roses were in their splendour,
Radiating beauty in white and crimson,
Bowing to the dawning sun.
We walked and walked, our feet on the green
Meadow giving velvet touch,
Innocent children were singing somewhere in unison
Peacocks in the background giving beautiful display.

There was a majestic scene of Life Tree,
Cluster of tall and straight nagphalli trees
Undaunted to the sun rays' direction

---

* A group of friends mesmerised by yellow-coloured flowers

Multi-layered, each flower bubbling with life.
We approached very close to the happy plants,
Astonished to see nature's wonder:
Bottom layers had shed flowers all around in the sand,
Whereas in the mid-layer they blossomed
In splendid magnificence
Perfume radiating, beauty all around,
Honey bees filling the flower bed, mutual love flowing.
Intoxicated with the scene, we looked at the top layer
Ring of the buds about to blossom
And new layers at their birth.

Again the great divine echo rang all around us:
'Flowers blossom, radiate beauty and spread perfume
And give honey. On the eve of life
Flowers silently fall to the earth, they belong.
Oh my creation this is the mission of human life
You are born, live a life of giving
And bond with ties of affection.
Your mission is the Life Tree.
My blessings to you my creation.'

Oh my human race
Let us sing the song of creation.

14 January 2001

O Almighty, bless us with knowledge.

A meeting was held quite far from Earth. 'It's time again for another birth,' said the angels to the Lord. 'This special child will need much more love. His progress may seem very slow, accomplishments he may not show, and he will require extra care from those he meets down there. He may not run or laugh or play; his thoughts may seem quite far away; in many ways he won't adapt, and he'll be known as handicapped. So let's be careful where he's sent, we want his life to be content.

'Please, Lord, find parents who will do a special job for him. They will not realize right away the major role they're asked to play. But with this child sent from above comes a stronger faith and richer love. And soon they'll know the privilege given in caring for this gift from heaven. Their precious charge, so meek and mild, is heaven's special child.'

O Almighty, Light the Lamp of Knowledge

Almighty we are your own creation
To you we bow and pray.
Light the lamp of knowledge
So that your blessings flow forever,
Like perennial rivers and dazzling sea waves.
O creator of the universe, fill our lives
With the choicest blessings of your heart.

O Almighty, light the lamp of knowledge.

The love of my mother embraces me
And the ascetic fervour of my father seeking endlessly your
    light
Transforms the yearning tears of my mother
Into glittering reflection of my ambition.
Grant solace to the pains of my father, Almighty,
By granting us a new life and beautiful smile.
You are the creator, you the sustainer.

O Almighty, light the lamp of knowledge.

Like other children we want to study and learn,
We too want to run and play like others,
In groups we want to sing and dance,
We want to hoist the national flag
On Independence Day.

O Almighty, light the lamp of knowledge.

We want to present our offerings as gratitude
For our teachers and revered father

We want to work and work for our nation
With our sweat enrich the great land of ours.

O Almighty, light the lamp of knowledge.

O Almighty enter our soul,
Bless us, so that we may live a life like that of others,
Let our life be beautiful like flowers,
As you are the fountain of life
Who creates ceaseless beauty.

Light the lamp of knowledge, O Almighty.

Almighty you created the earth and gave life,
Created the sun and gave light,
Sun rays like your blessings played on our heart,
Brought beauty of spring and took away autumn.
Almighty you gave a new life, gave light.

O Almighty, light the lamp of knowledge.

Armed with knowledge we dream and rise to thank you,
We pray, we bow, we worship for your grace,
Like clouds fill the water cups of the river,
You have kissed our life with music.
Now your sunshine greets us with a smile.

O Almighty, you lit the lamp of knowledge.

Original in Tamil composed after my visit to Central Institute of Mental
Retardation, Trivandrum, 28 May 2000.

Almighty, bless me always to be
With great teachers
Of high thinking.

Whenever I hear of communalism and social inequity, I vividly recollect an incident from Rameswaram Elementary School. I was in the fifth standard. A new teacher had come to our class. I always used to sit in the front row along with my close friend Ramanathan. The teacher could not comprehend a Brahmin boy and a Muslim boy sitting together. In accordance with the social ranking as perceived by the new teacher, I was asked to go and sit on the back bench. I felt very indignant and so did Ramanathan. Even today, the image of Ramanathan crying in class when I changed my seat to the rear row remains vivid in my mind. When this incident was related to our respective fathers and family friends, the teacher was summoned and told by them that what he had done was a snake's work. The strong convictions of our parents reformed the teacher half a century ago.

Harmony

Cranes and seagulls were wandering the sky,
Sea waves laughing and teasing the shore.
Musing my school days my mind leapt five decades,
A small school in Rameswaram town...

Hindu or Muslim, mosque or temple,
None of those divisions nagging the thinking;
Ramanathan and I, weaving words together,
Harmonious delight of Creator's children.

Suddenly a storm arrived unannounced.
Turbaned and tweedy, known as new teacher,
Asked us to sit away awkwardly from each other.
My tears dripped; Ramanathan wept,

Nor did we get the meaning of that separation.
Sunbeams saw through the sorrowful mood,
Silently lighting our tears into gems.
Creator of all, aren't You there?

Who is this one separates us here?
Years rolled by... yet we remained friends,
Sharing the sorrows and joys of yore.
The so-called educated separate our souls,

Sowing the seeds of discord and poison.
They give not knowledge but hate and defeat;
Tell others not to heed their unwanted advice,
As the Almighty created all equal and free.

At one with nature.

Agni, the intermediate range missile we had been working on for the past several years, was on the launch pad at Chandipur-on-sea. We were to launch it the next day. I was going from the launch pad to the Control Centre for the Launch Authorization Board. I was in a pensive mood, as problems had arisen in the last two attempts. However, we drew satisfaction from the fact that we could keep the missile intact. As I looked out through the window of the car I saw lilies of different colours blooming in the pools of water along the road. I got down to admire their dance in the morning breeze, leaning forward to try and touch them in their rapid motion. The interlude filled my heart with peace and all the tension melted away. I was ready to face challenges afresh. Next day Agni was launched. The rest is history.

Pursuit of Happiness

I was on an unbeaten path,
All around me were joyous flowers.
My familiar world appeared strange,
In the wild were growing treasures of nature.

Blooming flowers of bounteous beauty,
Vibrant colours, dancing in abandon.
Some were buds, others older,
Some on way to sought after liberty!

Men may make merry of flowers,
Children may make playthings of them,
Dismember them or ignore to dust,
Yet all these flowers embody a truth:

Beauty of consciousness trapped in peace
Blooms of flowers show Almighty in deed.
Sowing happiness, or solemnity in need
To express ourselves everywhere we need,

To offer them to God or to the beloved,
A touch of them makes all humans go tender.
Ah, that conscious beauty of marvellous peace,
In pursuit of happiness always we need.

My father, my mother,
I am your child.

Republic Day of 1990 brought a pleasant news. The President
of India had conferred Padma Vibhushan on me. I filled my
room with music. The music transported me into another
time, another place. In my mind I visited Rameswaram,
hugged my mother. My father ran his caring hands through
my hair. Jalaluddin announced the news to the crowd gathered
in the Mosque Street. Pakshi Laxman Sastry put a tilak on my
forehead. Father Solomon blessed me with his hand at the
holy cross on his locket. I saw Prof. Vikram Sarabhai smiling.
The sapling he planted twenty years ago was bearing fruit.
My heart was filled with gratitude.

Gratitude

Growing forest, groves on ascent,
Dangling fruits of branching trees,
Like toddlers clinging to fingers of mothers:
Blooms in bushes or muddied children?

Humming bees setting the tune,
Like unseen hands on veena strings.
Lions and deer, panthers and boars,
Wandering the forest like people on work,

Birds taking wing like children riding aeroplanes...
And spring waved a magic wand
Forests bloomed like heaven's yard
And days floated on a sea of dreams.

Then, like sudden clouds full of rumbling and thunder,
Disease and death descended upon the scene.
Panther and boar, all fell dead in heaps,
Death striking at will, like lightning gone haywire,

Wreaking havoc wherever it strikes.
Big or small, death never spared.
When just ten were left, they took to praying,
Remembering the Lord in reverberating faith.

Benign God in divine grace,
Mercifully appeared for the meek and praying,
And they could see the Almighty in glory.
All of them knelt and prayed and prayed.

God asked the cause of the prayer.
'Give us life, wipe out despair,' they cried.
And God's glance cured them all.
Astonished to find all of them well again,

Nine ran away with happiness writ large,
Just one was left to say Thank you' to the Lord!

Prayers, prayers everywhere
To relieve the pain.

The image of God as engraved on my mind by my father was that of an omnipotent being whom I must obey, upon whom I could call in times of distress, and who was the only source of ultimate happiness and peace. I always needed God to come out of despair. When I heard that Mother Teresa was in hospital (in 1991), I felt anguished and sat down to pray to the Almighty for her recovery. The prayers of many reached Him and she recovered to serve humanity once again.

Anguish

Wind is wild and water is troubled,
Lengthening night, desolate and dark,
Stars mimicking glowworm's lamp,
Standing in emptiness for anyone to care.

Angry lightning and fury of sky,
My heart in anguish wants to cry,
Why is it so? Mother Teresa in pain—
She who loves all His children!

Cares for them like a mother from her soul,
Her heart is home for those who have none.
Why is she ill? Who will care for our sick?
Who will then adopt all those left?

Who will take the wanderers home?
Tattered clouds in a sorrowful sky,
And the rain pouring like heaven in tears,
Nature too in pain, let us all pray,

Asking the Almighty to leave her on earth
To care for His children a little while more.

Man's will can transform rocky terrain into a blooming garden.

I had visited Imarat, Hyderabad in 1975. I experienced a feeling which I experienced earlier at Swami Sivanand's ashram in Rishikesh. The entire Imarat area was charged with intense vibrations. The rocks scattered around everywhere appeared to have tremendous energy contained within them. A sense of familiarity with the place overcame me. I felt as if I belonged there, though I had never visited it before. I left the centre in an emotionally charged state of mind. On a visit in 1981, after six years, I saw the place bubbling with activity, and was struck by the harmony in which man, nature and science seemed to be. Whenever I am in Imarat, the flowers, the trees and the rocks talk to me as if trying to convey a message.

Nature

Bright blue sky, at RCI* that day
My thoughts were soaring on freedom,
Hope was their strand in radiance of peace,
Hillocks were spotted in embracing clouds,
Scientists were working, silently, heads down:

Some will be great, and others part of greater works.
Finding the life around perfectly synchronized,
I asked myself: Who is the one controlling them all?
If that be God, where is He now?
Walking through that playful breeze,

I found a few squirrels valiantly gazing;
A golden bird just closed in on jasmines,
As though to talk the secrets of that hour.
I paused to ponder the blossoms of God,
Found them hinting finer new meanings.

Some were showing the signs of God,
Some others revealed part, yet others completely withheld.
Endeavours to grow, can they ever be in vain?
In a while, a robin enquired my search.
Enthused, I said: 'Indeed God!'

---

*Research Centre, Imarat, Hyderabad.

Swiftly taking off it said: 'You may not find here.'
Saw in its direction, myriad colours of evening clouds,
Setting sun and temple bells added meaning to the scene.
'Where is God?' an unknown voice spoke,
'Why not you look for Him, up in the orchard?'

Trees were still, and retreating light,
Birds were trying get back to nests,
Fruits were showcasing sweetness possessed,
Flowers were conveying secrets of creation.
Even glowing street lamps could not show me an answer.

My mind was on its wings,
As if trying to search the source of spring.
Softened and tired, I started for home,
Suddenly a flower fell on my head,
Started to speak and said:

'O creator of dreams,
Why do you keep searching for God?
Nature is His home, purity His abode
And Life is but His blessing!
Keep loving nature and care for its beings,
Then you can see divinity all over!'

Where there is hatred
Let me sow love.

—*St Francis of Assisi*

I came back to Hyderabad by the evening flight. Hyderabad was reeling under one of its worst riots. On my way from the airport to Kanchanbagh, I found only people in uniform on the roads. My heart was full of pain. Why such hatred? The boundary of recognition between man and beast is the heart that loves and cares for each other. Where is that heart? One day when death will knock at our door, what message will we have for Thee? What answer we will give Him for His kindness? We have no time to lose. There is still time to earn His grace.

God

The days were silent as if afraid of night,
Life receded like a fire without fuel
And joy and happiness just went extinct.
Was it a dance of death or annihilation?

Streets were empty, and roads were alone,
Sounds of weapons and shoes shook them all.
Men were out to kill brethren with cruelty:
Riots had broken the cage of peace and faith!

Satan was seen singing all around
As if rejoicing in His creation's misery
Ten thousand Hindus and as many Muslims
Said to have perished in tearful tragedy.

All of them were told: 'You are dying
For Khuda and Bhagwan.'
Littered bodies and liberated souls
Set out to search their saviour God.

Twenty thousand souls torn from life
In search of their Lord.
Darkness of sins spreading all over,
Yet He couldn't be traced.

For eons the souls were engaged in travel
Eager to see a glimpse of their God.
Some of them were searching for Allah,
Rest of them were reaching for Bhagwan.

When suffering made them sulking and humble,
Suddenly there was the Light of Lord,
'Surely it is my Khuda—'
'No, no! It is our Bhagwan.'
So started a chaos all over.

Suddenly a sound thundered from Light,
'I am none of yours! All ye hear!
Love was my mission and you spent it on hatred,
Killing my delight, stifling life.

'Know ye all: Khuda and Ram
Both are one, blossoming in love.'
Saying this the Lord thought for a while
Why did He make His creation so blind!

So he sent the souls back to earth
To spread the message of truth.
God is Love and Love is God
And a child was born all over again!

Dream, my friend, dream.

Your willingness to draw upon your inner resources—specially your imagination—and to undertake any task from your own unique standpoint makes you human. As with everyone else on this planet, you were sent by Him to cultivate all the creative potential within you and to live at peace with your conscience. You can claim your birthright to be a person only if you are willing to take the risks involved in ignoring all outside pressures to do things. The Greek philosopher Pythagoras said: 'Above all things, revere yourself.'

Message

The word water cannot quench thirst
And a formula cannot float a ship,
Mere mention of rain will not get you wet,

But the desire that stems from head and soul,
Pure and intense professes God's will,
Like eternally unbroken promise of spring,
Manifests into reality as imagined...

Confidence in one's ability is like fire,
Like vibrating frequencies all in resonance.
Seek the truth and the truth shall set you
    free,
You wish and work like seekers of truth.

Intensity of faith can destroy all obstacles.
Remember: All men are equal and created alike
And the Creator endowed them with inalienable
    rights
To life, to freedom, and to continued
    happiness.

And the clue to the mystery of
    success:
Love for your work and
    faith in your dreams,
There is no force on earth
    that can shatter your
    dreams!

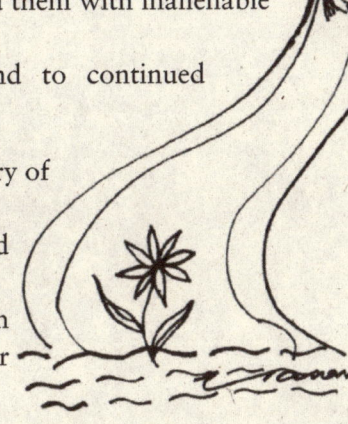

If you can give your son or daughter only one gift, let it be enthusiasm.

—Bruce Barton

My father, Avul Pakir Jainulabdeen, taught me a great lesson when I was a young boy. I was reading my lessons loudly at home by the light of the kerosene lantern when there was a knock at the door. Someone entered and asked for my father. When I told him he had gone for namaz, he said, 'I have brought something for him. Can I keep it here?' I called out to my mother for her permission: as she was also at namaz there was again no response. I asked the man to leave the package on the cot and continued with my studies.

My father was at the time chairman of the Rameswaram Panchayat Board. When he returned and saw the package, he said, 'What is this? Who has given it?' He opened the package. Inside was a costly dhoti, an angavastram, some fruits and sweetmeats. He was enraged. It was the first time I saw him so angry, and also the first time that I got a beating from him. Later, seeing me frightened and crying, he came and affectionately touched my shoulder. 'Never receive a gift; a gift is always accompanied by some purpose,' he advised, and quoted from the scriptures, 'When the Almighty appoints a person to a position, he cares to see that he is provided for. If a person takes anything beyond that, it is an illegal gain.'

I am in my seventies now, but the lesson learnt is still vivid in my memory.

Let It Be We

As a gardener plants seeds
My parents sowed a few lessons—
Transparent honesty, self-discipline,
Faith in goodness and sea-deep kindness.
Seed turned to flower, becomes the fruit
And my mind and body reap those lessons!

Looking at the world I see humans' lust for gold
Fighting each other, forgetting God,
Blind men looking for benign helping hand,
A small child on a stormy road struggling to cross,
Demonic pollution and defiled life.
If these be progress, what have we done?

What did we plant and what are we reaping?
Fifty years gone by since my father was headman.
Flattering people brought heaps of fruits.
Throwing them out, father taught me a lesson:
'Bad seeds should not be allowed to grow,
Weeds like this will have to go.'

Whose duty is it, to uproot the weeds?
Sacrificing self and braving the scandals,
Silently wiping unfolding untruths.
Why not me? Why me? If not me, who?
If not me, who?
And better still, let it be—We!

Imagine a beautiful thought
And live life.

'Where is heaven? you ask me, my child,—the sages tell us
it is beyond the limits of birth and death, unswayed by the
rhythm of day and night; it is not of this earth ....
The sea is beating its drums in joy, the flowers are a-tiptoe to
kiss you. For heaven is born in you, in the arms of the mother-
dust.'

        —Rabindranath Tagore, Lover's Gift

Poets give beauty and peace to our minds, enrich our
imagination and thereby our lives.

Clouds

Up in the clouds, absorbing thoughts!
All of them question me, Is this world real?
I am on the move glancing at these clouds
Sometimes in planes, otherwise in thoughts.

Scattered clouds are like clusters of buildings.
In the fairies' town of bluish sky.
Angels could be shaping these structures,
Occasionally crackling lightning to cheer the gods
Or pouring the rains to bolster our hopes!

The sun rays spread like blessings of gods
In coloured strands of flowers of heaven,
And those darkish clouds and their winding tunnels
Awaken me and make me realize myself in reality.
Yes, there is reality of power and fame too!

All these lead to familiar questions—
Where do we come from and why did we originate?
What kind of destination motivates us all?
Reminds me of my father, reciting Gibran to mother...

'Your children are not your children.
They are the sons and daughters of life's longing for itself.
They come through you but not from you...'
Ah! I wish that cloud's freedom for me!

To wander the horizons of limitless destiny,
To inhale and float in ascetic peace,
To detach from the drama of wooing for power,
To pray for love and peace of humanity.

Great thoughts will yield miracles.

The word 'memory' contains two words, 'more' and 'me'. If you could only remember more, you could have more of yourself. It is said, 'Seek the truth, and the truth shall set you free.' The steps towards seeking the truth are wanting, wishing, needing and deserving. Having taken these steps, if your desire to know is sincere and intense, not just idle curiosity, flashes of memory will lead you into the realm of self-discovery and help you overcome problems. Once you hold on to such memory, you will be led to your dream. The Bible says, 'Ask and you shall receive.'

Pride

Selfish world, starves us in need,
Manipulative men meaner in treatment.
Whenever I hear complaints of this breed,
Cosmic reality becomes my reply:
'In give and take; give comes first.
Start with giving and receiving shall follow!'
So do I say to the complaining world.

There was a time that we all saw
When propriety and pride were seated at back.
Then daylight dawned; emerged an era
'We aren't afraid; nor do we bow down,'
Half-clad Gandhi announced with conviction.
These words would make sense to those who're strong.

This world is like maya not centred on poles,
Age-old truth says that fittest shall survive,
And so will our might; as weak would just vanish.
Therefore my message to youth of this day:
'Free yourself from pessimistic distrust
Blessed by God arise to reach new heights.'

It is a wise father that knows his own child.

—William Shakespeare

When I was a child, my father used to take me for namaz. When he was kneeling to offer prayers, I used to repeat the words at random. Many a time my elder brother, Mustafa Kamal, used to correct me. In later days, during every journey from Rameswaram, my father would take me to the same mosque even when I was twenty-five. One day I saw a tear in my father's eyes as we parted. The tear demanded love of the grandchild.

Ancestor's Desire

Serenity of slumber yet floating in dreams,
I hear the voices of my endearing parents,
Up from the heaven as though looking down,
All the time they ask the question of succession.
Where is our grandson, to carry the mantle?
You made us proud; and it should go further...
Who will remember us when you also leave?

Choked in voice and muted in reply,
I never had an answer to render.
In pursuit of life sun lights up the days,
Cycle of days merges into morrows,
Yet parents' souls, their pleadings of yore,
Leave me pondering day after day,
Ancestor's pride and wherefore my life!

Towering dynasties have tumbled in history,
As great rulers' offsprings tore up their banner.
Each one is remembered for actions of self,
Like ferrying wind carries the fragrance of source,
And a fresh breeze floats my nagging dreams now
This breeze is all for a valiant new order:
And a fiery Agni pierced the sky.

An order of strength and thundering might,
Freedom from fear illumines the lives.
Traditional shackles—shaken down like fruits,
Sweet slumber and floating dreams render,
No more questions of ancestor's pride

And a beautiful night of fragrant breeze,
Peace is reigning and moonlight pouring.

And my parents appeared in my mind.
Their faces had smiles, and there were tears in their eyes.
They blessed me now with all their grace.
For gift of this grandson and symbol of strength
Agni, and for continuing their name.

Multiples of oil lamps
Give birth to light.

The success of Agni had put our country in a state of ecstasy. During the integration of Agni, an incident took place. A scientist, who was an expert in integration, had called up his home in Hyderabad from the site to ascertain if everything was all right. By then, he had been away for over forty days at a stretch from his home and family. His wife did not sound very clear on the telephone and the line was transferred to his father, who assured him that everything was fine and wanted to know when he would return home. A few days later, having just returned from a successful launch, he found his wife crying: to his dismay he found out that his wife's brother had died a week earlier in an accident. The family had not informed him for fear of disrupting his work on Agni.

I bow before the families with hands folded.

Unseen Hands

Far away in the Bay of Bengal,
Where sea is deep and waves are high,
Agni lands with glory and light,
Awakening the nation with acquired strength.

As the world in awe praised doyens of deed
Landed Agni, now surrounded by sea creatures
Curiously asking the source of its origin:
'Who made you Agni, and who shaped you Agni?

'Who all were behind this scintillating feat?'
Pondered Agni, gasping a while,
And delving into the past decided to speak:
'Scientists and engineers sweated it out,

'Silently merging many a day into night!
Making each part and testing my systems,
With care and delight of a creator's vision,
Hunger and sleep were submerged in mission!

'With enthusiasm and dedication in action
Melted their desires in making me alive.'
'So well the scientists made you in such fashion,'
Sea creatures quipped—in conversation!

Agni replied: 'No, not alone my friends,
Though motivation and desire are components of success,
Woven in heady mix of hard work and technology;
Yet, wives and mothers of my creators also

'Never allowed any problem to pierce my makers' hopes
And prayed in silence for success with lighted lamps
And they lighted the lamps every day to keep up the hopes,
Hopes of millions merged with blessings of these women.

'Beloved's love and affection of offspring,
Blessings of elders and glow of lamps lit by creators' wives;
I came out of the light that was quite bright
With hope, vision and love.

'When men and women are together
Love and understanding are created
Lamp of hope and creativity blossoms
And Agni with purity and strength emerges

'Nation grows, pride and prosperity bloom.'
Agni looked around, took a deep breath
And announced to those who were there all around,
'I emerged from the lamps lit by the mothers and wives of my
    creators.'

A lesson in true education.

My father had two friends, Father Bodel and Lakshmana Sastrigal. When I was around ten, I often found them discussing the Bible, Koran and Gita. My father was a custodian and the head of the local mosque. Pakshi Lakshmana Sastrigal was the vedic scholar of Rameswaram and head priest of the famous temple there and Father Bodel was the founder of Christ Church of Rameswaram. I think I got the best of learning from them, watching these three enlightened souls sit and discuss about the love and compassion of religions. For me they are the most important learned role models who taught me how a religion could be transformed into spirituality. These three great minds belonging to three religions working together in a small village had provided the foundation for promoting unity of minds for generations to come.

Rock Walls

Some build rock walls all their lives,
When they die miles of walls divide them.
Others build rock walls, one rock on another,
And then build a terrace, where they pray for love!

Yet others build walls to enclose orchards,
Endeavouring to find ways to fulfil hunger.
A few others build rock walls to make a home
It is their mission to serve humanity and nature.

I build no walls, to confirm joy or sorrow,
To sacrifice or achieve, to gain or lose.
I just grow flowers on all open spaces
And float lilies on ponds and rivers.

I keep planting trees, for birds to have nests.
At the dawn of the sun, when morning breeze blows,
Sunlight gets filtered through shining tree leaves.
Birds' flight gives me sense of freedom and pleasure,

Scattered light of colour and treasure,
Fragrance of flowers gives me delight of creator,
Lilies dancing to nature's rhythm!
Why should I build walls to confine them all?

I have no house, only open spaces
Filled with truth, kindness, desire and dreams:
Desire to see my country developed and great,
Dreams to see happiness and peace abound.

God's blessings await our efforts.

We fight for supremacy, assert our greatness, make ourselves unhappy as too others. We forget that in the overall scheme of things we are quite small really. We belong to a small galaxy, the Milky Way, and our Sun is a tiny star. Our habitat, Earth, is one of the most insignificant planets.

His Best Creation

God, the Almighty decided once
That the time had come to create human life.
Millions and millions of years were spent
In designing and developing that image
With mud and clay yet with mind in its place.

At last He made a shape of that image
And worked on and on striving for perfection.
Space-time and its multi-dimensional flow
Galloped and swallowed quite a great reach
And He decided that the image was ready, void of flaw,

It was time to give life to that being.
When Moon and the Sun were together seen shining
And all the stars were pouring their coolest rays
God commanded life to the man
And, he opened his eyes and smiled at the Lord.

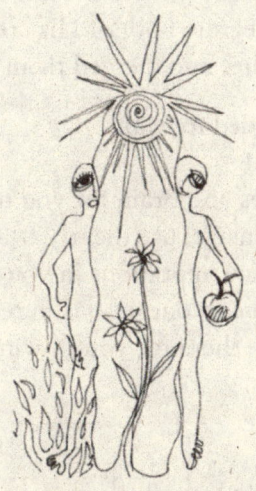

Ray of that smile made Almighty happy.
Meanwhile the man said: 'O Almighty, thank you.'
God was pleased at the first actions of man
And the man in God's image arrived here to stay.
Suddenly God had a surprising feeling

That something was missing in the man He made.
In flash of a second He created a fire
And Satan emerged from the flames in no time.
Satan too bowed in reverence to God.
The Almighty said: 'O Satan, my second creation,

'Bow before man the best of my creations.'
Defiantly Satan said: 'O my creator!
I may never bow before man;
I came from fire and he came from just clay
And why should I bow before him?

'Rather he also took millions of years for a shape...'
God for the first time had a problem in hand
And pondered this issue just for a while
Then decided to integrate both of His creations
He held them together and merged them into one.

Then God commanded to Man:
'O my best creation!
I have given faculties and brain for you to deploy
Endowed with my image, use them
To defeat the Satanic temptations in you
And then come to me as one who is pure
My blessings will be there for you to win.'

Sea is part of my life
Her waves are rhythm of my heart.

I was born in Rameswaram, an island in the Bay of Bengal. When I was at home, the sea would be roaring in different rhythms at morning, evening and night. Even the roar was different in different seasons. My father started building a sailing boat with a carpenter as his partner. I was with him, an eight-year-old. I saw it grow year by year. When it was launched after four years, a special namaz was conducted and the poor were fed. For ten years the boat provided a good livelihood. The expenses on my early education were met from the boat. One day a cyclone swept over Rameswaram island and the boat disappeared. Again that sorrow was combated with a namaz by my devout father.

Memory

When I flip through the pages of my boyhood
They get tossed about like Wordsworth's daffodils,
Angelic beauty of nostalgic seize
And beautiful spring flowers dancing in breeze.

Bluish sea waves breaching the golden shore,
With silvery foam dressing their leaping fine hands.
My father was crafting a seafaring boat
And we used to walk on the Rameswaram beach.

Taste of that padani still sweetens my soul,
Booming conch shells and pilgrims' pious walk
Act like fragrant breeze of divine hearts in motion
And my father still concentrating on carving his boat.

Piece after piece he works on the boat form,
Like praying to achieve divinely fine art.
Shoots of the seed, nature blossoms to flowers;
His craft was in unison with sea waves and nature.

The floating boats, the surging waves,
Widening horizons and breathtaking sky,
All of them were one and alike in his eyes:
Boats are just playthings for those who venture to sea.

Fish and sea creatures surrounding that boat
To appreciate the art and kiss on its forehead.
Sea, birds, fish and humans are all but one
And they just share the sea home on earth.

Fifty years later, the scene is quite different.
Fine art isn't created but just manufactured,
Soul of the creator nor does it manifest.
Humans and nature got separated somewhere…

Motorboats dissecting the heart of the sea line,
Driving the fish hordes terrified all around.
Even the sun dawns here fearing the fog,
Like a frightened child scanning featureless darkness.

Who will merge humans to peace of the Lord?
Nature and humans were created together,
Together they can govern this world,
Then only peace and bliss will be here!

The Great Star in sky has to be the focus of one's life.

I was walking on the historic shore of Srirangapatnam, where two battles took place in the eighteenth century. India made the world's first war rocket. These rockets are in the British War Museum—small tubes with gunpowder, tiny nozzle and warhead (a curved sword). Use of these rockets defeated the British. I mulled over the milestones and their interpretations as the dawn cleared the fog.

Tumult

Silvery fog veiled the expansive sea,
Sun yet to rise to scatter the challenge,
Yet, like caged children's fearful cry,
Roar of the sea pierced the veil of fog.

Autumn's dreariness all over the place,
Asking me to account for all my gone years,
Loneliness compounding chaotic thoughts,
I mull over most of the milestones of the past.

Rohini in orbit and soaring of Akash,
Agni and Prithvi with Nag and Trishul,
All of them tore into targets aflame,
Yet, did they pour upon us the showers of joy?

Who will be judging my soul-driven feats,
Scientist or historian or will I have to do?
Was it an effort of uplifting science,
Or verily armouring the country in space
With weapons of destruction to wipe out the race?

Nestless eagle soaring in sky,
All alone pondering on wanderings of life,
I too shall tackle that mutinous thought
With the pinpoint sharpness of eagle's sight.

Loneliness, anxiety and guilt that we feel
Strewn with frustration and sadness, leaving us sore
Are born with the bliss that we meet in this life.
Wisdom and challenges that courageous meet

Nurture heroes and make them great
Nor did I ever move fearing the fate.
All that I aspired was just a place
In hallowed portals for my homeland.

Like unbroken promise of rising sun,
Call of this noble deed made me to sweat.
I remain...and shall move over and ahead
Learning from losses in destiny's route.

Cheering my soul I saw dawning of sun
That scattered the fog and mutinous thoughts.
Prismatic spectrum of beauties in sky,
And I will have hyper plane to soar in that sky!

There are times when God asks nothing of his children except silence, patience and tears.

—C.S. Robinson

Tears

My tears glitter in moonlit nights,
My tears glitter in the darkest of dark night,
My tears glitter even in the hot mid-day sun,
My tears glitter in success and failure,
My children be brave, tears will make you great.

There is no God like mother.

In my boyhood, one night to the envy of my brothers and sisters I slept in the lap of my mother. Later in the night, I woke up when my mother's affection-filled tears fell on my cheeks. The memory remains fresh in my thoughts.

My Mother

Sea waves, golden sand, pilgrims' faith, Rameswaram, Mosque
    Street, all merge into one,
My mother!
You come to me like heaven's caring arms.
I remember the days of struggle when life was challenge and
    toil—
Miles to walk, hours before sunrise,
To take lessons from the saintly teacher near the temple.
Again miles to the Arab teaching school,
Climb the sandy hills to Railway Station Road,
Collect, distribute newspapers to temple city citizens,
And then going to school.
Evening, collect the money before study at night.
All this pain of a young boy.
My mother you transformed into pious strength
Kneeling and bowing five times a day
For the Grace of the Almighty. My mother,
Your strong piety is your children's strength,
You always shared your best with whoever needed the most,
You always gave, and gave with faith in Him.
I still remember a day when I was ten,
Sleeping in your lap
To the envy of my elder brothers and sisters.
It was full-moon night, my world only you knew;
At midnight I awoke to tears on my cheeks
You knew the pain of your child, my mother.
Your caring hands, tenderly removing the pain,

Your love, your care, your faith gave me strength
To face the world void of fear and with His strength.
We will meet again on the great Judgement Day, my mother!

God willed a happier world.

When people are happy or even in their distress, music and flowers are always friends of human beings. Particularly, good music enters into us and blossoms happiness in body and soul. With good music, wickedness in the minds of the people melts away in such a fashion that good human beings are born.

Whispers of Jasmine

Breezy dawn, crackling birds,
Jasmine grove my walking track,
Fragrance in the air of this noisy alley,
Creepers dancing to tunes of cuckoos,
Gust of wind threw a strand on the path

Taken aback just for a moment
Bees are back, just about their work
Even on the fallen jasmine flowers.
Dreading that I might tread on the creeper
Gently I take a circuitous route.

Whispers from creeper touch my soul,
Halting my gait caring to listen
Toddler bud talking to mother:
Why should we blossom asks that bud,
Plucked and treated shabbily by humans.

Hearing the child laughed the mother
Laughed and laughed and laughed:
Look, my child, why do birds sing,
See that lawn, peacocks dancing,
Jumping deer dancing to winds,

Water birds washing their feathers
As they go gliding fashionably on water—
All these beauties adding to scene.
Joyous nature's bounteous ways
Enable humans to listen to their heart.

If deer skip jumping and peacocks miss dancing,
Beautiful water birds duck their swimming,
Soulful music neither heard nor sung,
Fragrance of flowers and cheer of their colours,
If all we avoid, humans of earth

Harder in souls, harsher in tongue,
Violence pervading walks of life,
Abrasive thinking vicious in deed,
Disturbed homes, turbulence in world.
Wanting to ward off all these hells

God willed a happier world.
To the chiming beats of musical vibrance
Shehnai and sarod, veena and tabla
All these permeate and soften the soul
Just like dancing peacocks, singing parrots,

Jumping deer, gliding ducks
Smell of roses, daisy and lily,
Lotus and jasmine caressing the soul
Making the world a place to live
To mould humans, humane in deed.

But for nature hearts harden,
Wickedness permeates even the souls,
'Tis God's will gladden thy soul.
Blossom we will, blossom we will,
Cheer up, dear bud, blossom we will!

The power of prayer.

A young friend of mine suddenly had to undergo bypass surgery. The anxiety reduced him to tears. Just a while back he was considered so healthy and fit.

I wanted to cheer him. So, I assembled my thoughts and sent them to him. I asked him to look at this verse every day. Treatment is of the mind as much as the body.

Prayer Touches the Soul

My friend, a flamboyant youth, cheerful in spirit
Always dreaming of greater deeds
Bouncy in stride and of boisterous demeanour,
All assumed him to be hale and hearty.
Suddenly one day he turned sullen and grave,
The doctors prescribed bypass for his heart.

Silently he gazed at the valley from window
Budding tears moistened his eyes,
Family photo still smiled at him from wall
Squeezing his heart; he started crying.
I walked up to him and held him in peace,
Assembled my thoughts and asked him to read:

'When God is for me who can be against;
I sought the Lord, He heard me and delivered me from all
    fears;
Divine cure penetrates me, cures my pain,
Divine beauty enters into me, blossoms happiness in my body
    and soul
O Almighty, thank you for all the blessings you have poured!'
My friend read it once and repeated it many times.

Days rolled by, and I met him recovering,
Found my assembled thoughts pasted on bed
Cheerful as usual he handed me a note:
'Thank you my friend for elevating my thoughts

Your prayer cheered my body and soul,
My mind and body blossomed through strong heart.'
He held my hand and said, Thank you my friend.'

Not gold, but only man can make
A people great and strong.

—Ralph Waldo Emerson

In June 1989, I attended the Paris Air Show with some of my colleagues. Many types of aircraft made in different countries were executing complicated manoeuvres to show their special features. My heart yearned for my country and I scribbled this poem on a piece of paper.

Now we are a proud nation having successfully flown our own LCA (Light Combat Aircraft).

Soaring Dream

Fabulous air show of Paris in motion
My thoughts too in flight, and yearn for my nation
When will the planes designed in my land
Pierce the sky as lightning in action
And gracefully land like descending angels
All to the envy of spellbound spectators.
Yes we can, yes we can!
When we are all united in action and addicted to deeds
Sky can't be a limit for my nation in action.

Achieving glory.

After becoming the President the one state that I have visited a number of times is Bihar. I felt the youth of Bihar needed me. With the serene Ganges flowing through it, this beautiful land is full of spirits and a marvellous history. I have seen its youth to be unique in intellectual capabilities and hard work. They need to imbibe the pride of their state, which is full of opportunities. They need a vision to achieve their potential and glory.

I Am the Child of Bihar*

I am born in Bihar.

I live

I walk in the land where Lord Buddha walked.

I live in the holy land where Bhagwan Mahaveera lived.

I live in the happy land where Guru Gobind Singh walked and walked.

I study, I will study in the land where the great astronomer Aryabhatta discovered earth's orbit, sun's orbit and the dynamics of stars and planets.

The river Ganga smiles,

The fertile land of Bihar welcomes me for hard work.

In such a beautiful land, God is with me. I will work and work and succeed.

---

* I composed this poem while meeting children during a visit to Bihar in May 2003.

Angel is free because of his knowledge,
The beast because of his ignorance,
Between the two remains the son of man to struggle.

—Rumi

On 15 August 1947, my high school teacher, Rev. Iyyadurai Solomon, took me to hear the freedom at midnight speech of Pandit Jawaharlal Nehru. In those days, there were not many radios around. We were all moved to hear him. The next morning the newspapers announced the momentous event in banner headlines. But, alongside, ran another news item which is still embedded in my memory. It was about how Mahatma Gandhi was walking barefoot in Noakhali, to help assuage the pain of the families affected by communal riots there.

Normally, as Father of the Nation, the Mahatma should have been at the capital to see the transfer of power and unfurl the national flag. Instead, he was at Noakhali! Such was the greatness of the Mahatma. It left an everlasting impact on my mind.

My National Prayer

The grand scene of the birth of Independent India:
In that midnight, the flag of the ruler of two centuries
    lowered,
The tri-color fluttering at the Red Fort amidst National
    Anthem.
The first vision of Independent India dawned.

The rejoice everywhere, happiness all around,
There was a tender cry: where is the Father of the Nation?
The white-clothed soul walking in the midst of sorrows and
    pain,
Injected by hatred and ego, the result of communal violence.

The Father of the Nation, Mahatma, walking barefoot
In the streets of Bengal for peace and harmony
With the strength of the blessed soul of the Mahatma
I pray to the Almighty: When will be the dawn of the second
    vision?

Create thoughts in the minds of my people,
And transform those thoughts into action.
Embed the thought of Nation being bigger than
The individual, in the minds of leaders and people.

Help all the leaders of my country to give strength
And bless the nation with peace and prosperity.
Give strength to all my religious leaders to bring
Unity of minds among all our billion people.

O Almighty, bless all my people to work and transform
Our country from a developing into a developed nation.
Let this second vision be born out of the sweat of my people,
And bless our youth to live in a Developed India.